Blended And Loving It

Thirty-Day Devotional & Prayer Journal

Inspiration for Blended Families

By

Dr. Slavoski L. Wright Sr.

Umeka D. Wright

Copyright © Dr. Slavoski L. Wright Sr. and Umeka D. Wright, 2020

Cover image: © CJ Phillips Visuals

ISBN-13: 978-0-578-80077-6

Publisher's Note

Printed and bound in the United States of America. All rights reserved. No part of this book may be reproduced or transmitted in any form or by any means, electronic or mechanical, including photocopying, recording, or by any information storage and retrieval system except by a review who may quote brief passages in a review to be printed in a magazine, newspaper, or on the Web without permission in writing from Author Name.

Although the author and publisher have made every effort to ensure the accuracy and completeness of information contained in this book, we assume no responsibility for errors, inaccuracies, omissions, or any inconsistency herein. The advice and strategies contained herein may not be suitable for your situation. You should consult with a professional where appropriate. Neither the publisher nor the author shall be liable for damages arising here from.

This devotional is dedicated to:

Our six children: Kori, Slavoski II, Hannah, Braylon, Ryan and Dixon. You all taught us the meaning of Blended and Loving it. The journey with you has been an adventure of tears, laughter, fun and most of all intentional love. Continue to love one another intentionally, regardless of what is said by society. DNA, last names, and blood do not make us family, the love we have for one another makes us family. We are family and we will always be family.

CONTENTS

Introduction   9

PART I
The Marriage   11

Day One   13
What God Has Joined Together

Day Two   19
Keeping God In It

Day Three   25
No Outside Influences

Day Four   31
Not Half, Not Step, Just Family

Day Five   37
If God Is For Us, Who Can Be Against Us?

Day Six   43
Be The Example

Day Seven   49
On One Accord

PART II   55
Wife, Mom, Bonus Mom, Stepmom

Day Eight   57
Where Did You Come From?

Day Nine   63
Pray Without Ceasing

Day Ten   69
Finding Your Comfort Zone

Day Eleven   75
Intentional Love

Day Twelve   81
Fishbowl

Day Thirteen   87
For The Children

Day Fourteen   93
The Love You Give

PART III   **99**
Husband & Dad

Day Fifteen   101
Being Like Joseph

Day Sixteen   107
Can't Do It Alone

Day Seventeen   113
How Strong Can You Be?

Day Eighteen   119
Don't Quit

Day Nineteen   125
Test Of A Man

Day Twenty   131
Will She Leave Me?

Day Twenty-One
The Days To Come — *137*

PART IV — **143**
Children

Day Twenty-Two — *145*
Where Do I Fit In?

Day Twenty-Three — *151*
Together We Make A Family

Day Twenty-Four — *157*
Trusting God Through The Process

Day Twenty-Five — *163*
No Magic Pill

Day Twenty-Six — *169*
The Trying Times

Day Twenty-Seven — *175*
Choosing Sides

Day Twenty-Eight — *181*
For The Children

PART V — **187**
We are One

Day Twenty-Nine — *189*
Matching Hearts

Day Thirty — *195*
Blended And Loving It

About the Authors — *201*

INTRODUCTION

Blended and Loving It is a daily devotional designed to meet the spiritual needs of strengthening the nontraditional family. Love has a way of bringing things together, and through the love of God, your family dynamic is by His design. We encourage you to first stand on the love that God used to bring your families together, because it is the most powerful tool that God has given you. Then have the Faith to know that God is truly able to strengthen and grow your family and its bond. God is faithful and walks with the entire family every day. Finally, keep the hope of knowing that God is in control of it all. God led you to this devotional by design, and He wants your family to be led and carried by him. *"Three things will last forever—faith, hope, and love—and the greatest of these is love." 1 Corinthians 13:13 (NLT)*

This devotional will offer spiritual guidance, encouragement and motivation to individuals in blended families, newly blended families and soon-to-be blended families. The devotional consists of five sections; each section is dedicated to a member of the family. By the end of your thirty days, we pray that you have grown closer to Christ individually and collectively, and may your family be blessed because of it. Each daily devotional includes an inspirational story, scripture, and a place for you to insert your prayer or reflection with God.

Reflection

What do you hope to gain from this devotional?

_____
_____
_____
_____
_____
_____
_____
_____
_____

Personal Prayer

God I am trusting and believing you to do
_____
_____
_____
_____
_____ within my blended family…

PART I
THE MARRIAGE

Marriage is described by the word of God as a man and woman joining together in holy matrimony and two becoming one. The core values within your marriage will set the tone for your blended family. Throughout this section, the values of love, faith, commitment, determination and trust will be our focus. When you make the above values a priority within your marriage and family, you will be able to face any and everything that comes your way. When you and your spouse stand together and work together it is difficult for any type of divide to take place.

DAY ONE

WHAT GOD HAS JOINED TOGETHER

Scripture

Matthew 19:5-6 (NLT) "This explains why a man leaves his father and mother and is joined to his wife, and two are united into one. Since they are no longer two but one, let no one split apart what God has joined together."

The only relationship prioritized above marriage should be the one we have with God. When He is the center of a marriage, He will automatically become the center of a family. God brought Adam and Eve together as the first husband and wife. He formed Eve from Adam's rib, which shows us how men and women are to leave their father and mother and be joined together forever, inseparably (Genesis 2:24; Matthew 19:5). The stronger the marriage unit, the stronger the whole family will be.

Although the marriage may not be the first, it still holds the same affirmation of what God says about marriage and His commands. Fortunately, you become wiser the next time around. You are more equipped to handle marriage woes, (we pray that anyway). But when the marriage is grounded in God, everything will fall into place. Tests will come; however, if the marriage is firmly rooted in God and the Holy Spirit's guidance is being followed, the tests will be passed. Pray for each other daily, and watch God form a bond in the marriage that will help you battle all other things in such a way that you will rejoice mightily when it is attained.

Personal Reflection Prayer

Father, we pray that you allow your hand to move upon this marriage; that your guidance will be given unto to us to continue to draw closer to each other in love. We pray that you honor us with your presence and love each day and that we can give each other the love that you have given us. Cover and lead us through this day. In Jesus' name, Amen.

_____
_____
_____
_____
_____
_____
_____
_____
_____
_____
_____
_____
_____
_____
_____
_____

DAY TWO

KEEPING GOD IN IT

Scripture

Ecclesiastes 9:11 (NLT) "I have observed something else under the sun. The fastest runner doesn't always win the race, and the strongest warrior doesn't always win the battle. The wise sometimes go hungry, and the skillful are not necessarily wealthy. And those who are educated don't always lead successful lives. It is all decided by chance, by being in the right place at the right time."

For a marriage that has been truly blessed by God, you always have to hold fast to your faith in knowing that God will take care of each of you. It may not be that you have done something wrong as a couple, but that by design, things have come to make your marriage even stronger. Hold firm to the things that God has promised, especially that He will never leave you, nor forsake you. If you allow your marriage to stay strong as the three stranded cord (man, woman and God), the race can be won. Have a marriage that fights battles with each other, not one that battles against each other when troubles come. It just may be that season for you, that season of growth, not despair.

Personal Reflection Prayer

God, we pray that where we are, that you continue to be also. While we understand and know that trouble will come, we ask that when they arrive, that we are quickly reminded that we can't overcome them without you. Whether it be a good or bad day, we pray that you lead us through it, and we become greater by it because of you. In Jesus' name, Amen.

DAY THREE

NO OUTSIDE INFLUENCES

Scripture

Proverbs 3:5-6 (NLT) "Trust in the Lord with all your heart; do not depend on your own understanding. Seek His will in all you do, and He will show you which path to take."

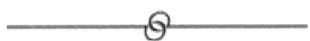

The dynamics of a blended family is entirely different than your traditional family. Blended families come with a host of family members and friends from the past and current relationships. There is more than just husband and wife. You usually have man, woman, children from each side, exes, ex's parents, and current in-laws.

With so many hands in the pot, things are bound to get messy. It is important to establish what is best for your family and stick to it. People will want to give you advice and share their thoughts. However, it is important to keep the outside influences outside of the home. God is the only influence that is needed when it comes to your family. Listening to too many people begins to cloud your judgment, and the interference can become overwhelming. Blended families are different and require different types of love, rules that are intentional and tailored to your family.

Personal Reflection Prayer

It's on this day that we need you to truly be our guide, God. We are putting our trust in you and only you to mend and mold our family the way that you desire for it to be. Bless us to lean only to your understanding and acknowledge you first. Where you lead God, we will follow. In Jesus' name, Amen.

_____
_____
_____
_____
_____
_____
_____
_____
_____
_____
_____
_____
_____
_____
_____
_____

DAY FOUR

NOT HALF, NOT STEP, JUST FAMILY

Scripture

John 13:34 (NLT) "So now I am giving you a new commandment: Love each other. Just as I have loved you, you should love each other."

In today's world, we long for the desire to put titles on everything and everyone in our lives. When it comes to our families, we should remain title free. Attempting to define everyone in the family complicates and makes things even more difficult. People often ask the kids, "Are you all real brothers and sisters?" And since we are real humans, the answer is YES. We are REAL brothers and sisters, Your relationship with one another is not determined by who has the same mom and dad or shares the same last name and DNA. Love makes a family - no need for half, step, or biological, just pure love. Do not allow society to define your family; you are defined by the love of God and the love for one another.

Personal Reflection Prayer

Now Lord, let us first feel your love, but most importantly, display your love. In our home, remind us that we are one. One family, one unit, because you look at our family as all yours. Just as you look at us as all yours, give us the mindset that we are all one in our hearts and minds. One family without titles but full of genuine love. In Jesus' name, Amen.

_____
_____
_____
_____
_____
_____
_____
_____
_____
_____
_____
_____
_____
_____
_____
_____
_____

DAY FIVE

IF GOD IS FOR US, WHO CAN BE AGAINST US?

Scripture

Ecclesiastes 4:12 (NLT) "A person standing alone can be attacked and defeated, but two can stand back-to-back and conquer. Three are even better, for a triple-braided cord is not easily broken."

"If God is for us, who can be against us?" (Romans 8:31, NIV) This scripture reminds us that no man can separate what God has joined together. God has not only joined you and your spouse together, but He has also formed and joined your families together. When those trials and tribulations arise, remember God's word and turn to Him for strength and guidance during the difficult times. When those difficult times come, stand together as a couple first, then as a family. You must face those difficult times together as a team. Satan seeks to destroy you and your family. Your family unit is stronger together. Weapons will form, but they will not prosper. Hold on to God's promising words, and fight for your family.

Personal Reflection Prayer

When the enemy attacks, God, we pray that we stand firmly on your Word together, for we understand that you have joined us together. Remind us that when we face adversities, it's in these moments that we stand together and meet them. For together we are stronger, and by your strength provided, we can overcome anything. In Jesus' name, Amen.

DAY SIX

BE THE EXAMPLE

Scripture

Mark 10:6-9 (NLT) "But God made them male and female' from the beginning of creation. This explains why a man leaves his father and mother and is joined to his wife, and the two are united into one. Since they are no longer two but one, let no one split apart what God has joined together."

"A pretty woman and handsome man will make a beautiful wedding. BUT a virtuous woman and a righteous man will make a beautiful marriage."

Marriage is more than just looking the part. It takes a true relationship with God to be able to really make a marriage be what God intended for it to be. Not only that, but it also takes the major effort of the husband and wife to apply those principles, even in the low and bad times.

What most people see is the surface of the picture that is portrayed. However, create a marriage that people can feel the presence of God when they see you together. Don't stop there, create a marriage that each of you feel the presence of God in each other and watch God take you to new and higher heights each day.

A righteous man and a virtuous woman are a combination that the devil can't ever win a battle against.

Personal Reflection Prayer

Lord, let someone see you through us. While we might not be where you want us to be, let us be the example for people to know what you are doing in us. Give us the determination to be more like you, God, and through that determination, our visual marriage can be seen, but we want your power to be felt. In Jesus' name, Amen.

_____
_____
_____
_____
_____
_____
_____
_____
_____
_____
_____
_____
_____
_____
_____
_____
_____

DAY SEVEN

ON ONE ACCORD

Scripture

Amos 3:3 (NLT) "Can two people walk together without agreeing on the direction?"

Wow! The power of knowing where we are going and being on the same page! Is it even possible to go forward without agreeing? When God made us one, He joined us together to be on one accord. Does that always happen? No, it does not. However, it's only for a moment; then we come together to get back on track. Isn't that a beautiful thing? To walk together in unity and not allow Satan to hold our attention for too long.

When we walk together, knowing what we want to accomplish in our family, we always find a way to achieve it. It's not solely by our efforts, but it's by the design of God. When we trust in Him and follow Him, we are already walking in the same direction. But when we show Him that we are on the same page, the new heights He will take us to are unimaginable. Without Him, we would be like a ship without a sail, so let us continue to live in this manner and always come together to know we are going where God wants us to go. Where He leads, we will surely follow!

Personal Reflection Prayer

Father, mend our hearts and minds together that you can lead us. Remove any division that may be trying to part us, for we understand that we can't do anything without you. So, we ask that you bless us to go in the same direction, the direction in which you lead us, for we want to walk with you and be on one accord. In Jesus' name, Amen!

_____
_____
_____
_____
_____
_____
_____
_____
_____
_____
_____
_____
_____
_____
_____
_____
_____
_____

PART II

WIFE, MOM, BONUS MOM, STEPMOM

This section of the devotional is dedicated to the hard-working moms, stepmoms, and bonus moms. For as long as I could remember, when people remarry, the word 'step' was added to your role, i.e. stepmom, stepdads, and stepchildren. Within this last decade, bonus mom, bonus dad and bonus children became a popular title. The word 'step' has received a negative connotation for years and if we are being honest, it still does to this day. The perception of a stepparent is not always a positive one, stepparents are usually thought to be mean, evil, or uncaring. Bonus, meaning extra or additional, gives a new and positive spin on an old title with the same meaning. It is all about perception. Regardless if you call yourself a stepmom or bonus mom, at the end of the day, we are all mothers working hard to blend our families and create some form of normalcy within our households.

Wearing the title of a stepmom or bonus mom is not an easy task. We are often overlooked, unappreciated, and picked on for being the newbie to the family. It will require hard work, dedication, perseverance, intentional love, and most of all, God. My faith in God is what has gotten me through so many trials and tribulations.

May God continue to bless you, your marriage, and your blended family.

DAY EIGHT

WHERE DID YOU COME FROM?

Scripture

Psalm 133:1 (NIV) "How good and pleasant it is when God's people live together in unity."

It quickly became a reality that although my soon to be husband and I were crazy about one another; our children and exes did not share the same excitement. Our small single families of one adult and two children were now merging and creating a large family of two adults and four children, and shortly after marriage, one child on the way.

Blending your family is a major adjustment for everyone, especially the children involved. While you may think as long as we love one another and treat everyone fairly, all will be well, there is so much more to it than that. In our case, God was at the forefront of our marriage and our family. We pray daily as a couple. We worship together and gather at the center of our home in a circle and pray as a family every Sunday. I believe that this is what closed those gaps and got us through the most challenging times of our lives.

So how can you get through those challenging times? Family meetings are a must when dealing with blending families. We held several family meetings early into our relationship to include the children. Everyone needs a voice in the family that they are a part of; that way, it answers those questions of where did these people come from.

Personal Reflection Prayer

Heavenly Father, I thank you for your faithfulness and your unconditional love. Thank you for joining this family together and giving us the strength to push through those difficult moments and providing us with the strength to fight for our family. Lord, we ask that you continue to bless this union and be a hedge of protection around our family. In Jesus' name, Amen!

_____
_____
_____
_____
_____
_____
_____
_____
_____
_____
_____
_____
_____
_____
_____
_____

DAY NINE

PRAY WITHOUT CEASING

Scripture

Philippians 4:6 (NIV) "Do not be anxious about anything, but in every situation, by prayer and petition, with thanksgiving, present your requests to God."

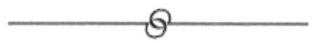

The same way you pray for your spouse, you should pray for your step/bonus children's biological parents. There is no magic pill or secret ingredient to blending your family, but I must tell you prayer was my saving grace. Prayer got me through some really tough days and nights. The Bible tells us to pray without ceasing, and I am living proof that prayer works.

In the midst of one of my own stepmom crises, I remember crying in frustration to my mother, and she said to me, "Have you prayed for them?" Well, of course I had prayed about the situation but I had not specifically prayed for them. She then said to me, "You need to pray for them daily, call their first and last names in prayer and ask God to touch their hearts and remove any negativity from your heart and their hearts, keep them safe and allow no harm to come their way, and whatever HIS will is, let it be done. She also asked, "If you are praying then why are you worrying? If you are praying, then don't worry and if you are worrying don't pray."

Listen, the last thing I wanted to do was pray for individuals that I felt had wronged me and that did not have my best interest in mind. I then thought to myself, *at this point, I am desperate and have nothing to lose but have everything to gain.* Pray even when you do not feel like praying. Those are the times you need to call on God the most. Prayer is essential and made a big difference in me and how I viewed situations, and most importantly, the way I responded to situations and individuals. A family that prays is one that believes in the power of prayer, so pray for your family and with your family.

Personal Reflection Prayer

Lord, I come to you praying that you touch my heart Lord, reveal and remove anything within me that is not like you, Lord. I come to you asking that you also touch the other adults' hearts (call their first and last name) involved in our blended family and remove any malice, hatred, and bitterness from us all. In Jesus' name, Amen!

_____
_____
_____
_____
_____
_____
_____
_____
_____
_____
_____
_____
_____
_____
_____
_____

DAY TEN

FINDING YOUR COMFORT ZONE

Scripture

Proverbs 3:5-6 (NLT) "Trust in the Lord with all your heart; do not depend on your own understanding. Seek His will in all you do, and He will show you which path to take."

No one likes to be uncomfortable or feel out of place in any situation, especially within your family and your own home. Blending and bringing two very different families together can sometimes be difficult and could cause several uncomfortable moments. It is important for your sanity, and all family members, to create a new normal for your family. Try not to focus too much on the outsiders; and by outsiders, I mean those outside of your blended immediate family. Your focus should be on yourself, your spouse, and the children involved. Create comfortability for your family and your household. Doing so will provide your blended family with a sense of peace and calmness in the midst of chaos.

Finding your comfort zone is the moment of knowing and understanding that you have all that you need within your family - realizing that when the family is bonded together with God's love, anything is possible. We are often reminded that a family that prays together stays together, a family that works together survives together, more importantly, together you are a family. Every blended family is different and will require different methods to properly blend. Turn to God when you are in search of your comfort zone and trust that He will guide and direct your family's path.

Personal Reflection Prayer

God, I trust you and believe that you have a plan for our family. I am leaning and depending on you during these difficult and uncomfortable times within my life. Lord, I am praying that you grant peace, strength, and comfort. In Jesus' name, Amen!

_____
_____
_____
_____
_____
_____
_____
_____
_____
_____
_____
_____
_____
_____
_____
_____
_____
_____
_____

DAY ELEVEN

INTENTIONAL LOVE

Scripture

Philippians 1:9 (NLT) "I pray that your love will overflow more and more, and that you will keep on growing in knowledge and understanding.

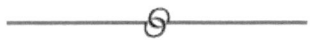

It is important to intentionally love one another. What I mean by that is no matter how upset you get, how hurt you are by the situation, and no matter how their biological parents treat you as an adult, you must show intentional love to your bonus children. Sometimes you have to go out of your way to show that you love your bonus children. It becomes a real-life action that speaks louder than words.

In most cases, children are caught in the middle, and they hear all sorts of stories, so it is your job as their bonus mother to show them unconditional love. The way you go about doing that is being consistent, open and loving and whatever they need for you to be to them at that time in their life. My way of showing intentional love to my bonus children is communication. I talk to them; they talk to me and we talk to one another. I ask questions and listen to them. When it is difficult for them to express themselves, I then ask probing questions such as *how does that make you feel,* or *what do you need from me?*

Even when your bonus children do not want to build a relationship with you, continue to be consistent, continue to show unconditional, intentional love. As the relationship grows they will see your actions rather than any words that have been spoken about or against you. When you find yourself in a negative place and those negative feelings begin to rise, this is when you must focus on intentional love. Intentional love is a reminder of what Christ would do at that moment; how would He respond. We all know He would respond in a manner of love and respect.

Personal Reflection Prayer

Heavenly Father, thank you for loving us when we do not deserve your love. Allow us to remember your love and love each other how you love each of your children. God grant us the ability to love our children and exes the way you love us. In Jesus' name, Amen!

_____
_____
_____
_____
_____
_____
_____
_____
_____
_____
_____
_____
_____
_____
_____
_____
_____
_____

DAY TWELVE

FISHBOWL

Scripture

Psalm 23:5-6 (NLT) "You prepare a table before me in the presence of my enemies; You anoint my head with oil; My cup runs over. Surely goodness and mercy shall follow me all the days of my life; And I will dwell in the house of the Lord forever."

Have you ever watched fish swim in a fishbowl? They circulate round and round in the same space, exploring the same things. They are living their lives on constant display in plain sight, nowhere to hide and nowhere to go. They appear content and unbothered by the world around them. Sometimes in a blended family you feel as if your life is like living in a fishbowl, on constant display. Someone is always watching, listening, and following how you and your family live your life. Early on within our blended family I was bothered by the fishbowl lifestyle but as time went on, I changed my perspective on how I viewed my fishbowl. When we as adults watch fish swim in a tank, we find ourselves daydreaming, thinking, relaxing and sometimes intrigued by the contents inside the tank. When children see a fish tank they show excitement, joy and fascination.

Although being watched may be bothersome, you never know the emotions that your fishbowl may be giving the person watching. Being watched is not always negative; allowing your light to shine publicly reveals to all that watch that God is in control. Remain unbothered and content while on display and cast all your cares on God. When you are walking in love and in obedience to God's word, no matter who tries to come against you, they cannot and will not stop the blessings that God has in store for you.

Personal Reflection Prayer

Lord, we are praying that you continue to receive the glory and that others will see your love through our family. In Jesus' name, Amen!

DAY THIRTEEN

FOR THE CHILDREN

Scripture

John 13:34-35 (NLT) "So now I am giving you a new commandment: Love each other. Just as I have loved you, you should love each other. Your love for one another will prove to the world that you are My disciples."

"The smarter you get, the less you speak," is an old Arabic Proverb that we hear often.

I try to take the time to process my thoughts, on how my words or actions will affect the intended individual and also how they will affect the children involved. Let's be honest, unfortunately as bonus parents we do not get the same leniency that the biological parents receive when it comes to our behavior. The biological parents' negative behavior may be overlooked because they are hurt or experiencing severe trauma from the break-up or struggling to accept a new person in their children's lives. As a bonus parent, we have to always watch our words, actions, facial expressions and anything else that can be perceived as negative.

Treat your bonus children the way you would want your biological children treated if they had a bonus mom. It is important to remember that your main focus is the children, do your best to block out any negativity and place your focus and energy on the wellbeing of the children. No matter the age the children are watching, and they will remember the behaviors of both parties later in life. What memories would you like to leave behind?

Personal Reflection Prayer

God, we thank you for the everlasting love you have shown our family. We pray, Lord, that you touch our hearts and our minds. In Jesus' name, Amen!

DAY FOURTEEN

THE LOVE YOU GIVE

Scripture

1 Corinthians 13:7 (NLT) "Love never gives up, never loses faith, is always hopeful, and endures through every circumstance."

As stated before, parenting and loving one another is intentional, but when it comes to step-parenting, you must be even more intentional. You are trying to prove that you are not the bad guy; you normally go above and beyond with your stepchildren, to the point where some may perceive that you are treating your stepchildren better than your biological children. Perception is reality and the last thing you want is for your stepchild to perceive that you don't like them or love them. The discipline is the same, but you have to be consistent and intentional about the love you give, or it could be misconstrued as the hate you give.

Personal Reflection Prayer

Thank you, Lord, for your continued blessing over our family. God help us to become and remained unified in your name. Help our family share the same vision, unity and love, the vision of understanding and forgiveness, and the vision of mercy and kindness. I pray that No weapon formed against my family will prosper. Lord block any tricks from the enemy and protect our home from division and discord. In Jesus' name, Amen!

PART III

HUSBAND & DAD

This section of the devotional is primarily dedicated to the husbands of blended families. There are many books and avenues for wives of the families to get support and read to help manage, but what seems to get lost in the shuffle are the husbands.

It is understood that wives are the more emotional ones by nature and most of the things that I have seen catered to the wives. However, what about the husbands? Are we not considered to be enduring just the same? When my wife hurts or something is not right, I feel the pain as well. It may be displayed a little differently, but that does not mean that we as men do not feel the pain. Who are the counterparts that experience a wife who is unhappy, depressed, sad, crying, hurting, disrespected, or just having a bad day? You guessed it, the husbands. The next few days of devotion are dedicated to the husbands. Take it, read it, meditate on it, and know that God has you covered just the same.

DAY FIFTEEN

BEING LIKE JOSEPH

Scripture

Matthew 1:24 (NLT) "When Joseph woke up, he did as the angel of the Lord commanded and took Mary as his wife."

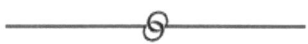

You entered into this marriage accepting the total package. Think about this - Joseph was actually in a blended family. A unique blended family, but a blended family, nonetheless. Joseph adhered to the words of God and accepted what had taken place. He had a hand in raising Jesus on earth. Perhaps you may have kids and/or your wife may have kids that you both merged. Jesus relied on Joseph as a child; just as such, ALL of your kids rely on you.

They watch your strength, your demeanor, your actions, and the person you ultimately are. It can be difficult at times, but it is by design, God's design, that you are now in their lives. Consider it an honor and not a burden that God led you to her. However, He didn't lead you to only her, He led you to them. Stand proud in knowing that you are chosen and be just like Joseph. You may not have the perfect little saint, but what you have is a grand opportunity to be that father that is needed.

Personal Prayer Reflection

Lord, you have placed me here first out of love and next for a purpose. Now, Lord, I pray that you give me the strength to fulfill that purpose to the glory and honor of your name. Grant me strength in times of weakness, peace in times of storm, and wisdom in times of guidance. In Jesus' name, Amen.

DAY SIXTEEN

CAN'T DO IT ALONE

Scripture

Isaiah 55:8 (NLT) "My thoughts are nothing like your thoughts," says the Lord. "And My ways are far beyond anything you could imagine."

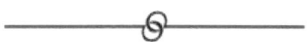

PRAYER CHANGES THINGS, seems to be a cliché bit of advice that is given, right? Hard to understand when you are seeking for that relief to come instantly. Prayer is essential, but also understand that being patient is essential as well. I know, another word that no one wants to hear. However, this is a marathon and not a sprint. As a man, you want it fixed and done right now, but this requires guidance from God. You can't do this alone. You will need God to help guide you in leading your family. You will need Him walking right beside you to make sure that the steps you have taken are by Him. When He orders your steps, know they will be the right steps and there won't be a need to come back and start over.

Think about the last thing you tried to fix or repair without following the instructions - did that come out perfect or did you have to backtrack some steps along the way? Following God will eliminate the backtracking and stop the devil from holding you back. Call on Him. Wait on Him. Be specific in your prayer and watch Him do it.

The proposal and saying, "I Do," was actually the easy part. Blending it all requires that added touch of making sure God is present. When you wait and watch Him work, you will truly experience the joy for the entire family. Follow Him!

Personal Reflection Prayer

God, give me the ability and desire to follow you. Help me to know that I can't do it alone, no matter how hard I try. Grant me the sense of patience, that I wait to hear from you and do what you say to do. Bless me as a man, a husband, a father, and the leader of my family that you require me to be. In Jesus' name, Amen.

DAY SEVENTEEN

HOW STRONG CAN YOU BE?

Scripture

Philippians 4:13 (NLT) "For I can do everything through Christ,[a] who gives me strength."

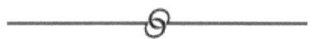

It's an incredible feeling to understand the leadership role that we have been given. It gives a great sense of pride and honor to know that we lead our families according to God's plan. However, it is not always easy. In fact, there are a lot of breaking moments that we as men have. We will never share those out loud, but on the inside, we are bearing them.

Our struggles magnify when we hear our wives' problems, our children's problems, and the strong men we thought we were, suddenly become men seeking strength and wondering how much we can truly carry to keep the family going. The complexities of learning how to manage it all, especially in a blended family, can be a weakening blow.

Remember this: nothing will come easy. The scripture is true that you can do all things through Christ that strengthens you. You just have to hold on to that and walk as though even the little strength that you have left is still enough to lead and guide the family. The devil wants you to think differently and tell you it's too much, but God joined us together with our wife, not by mistake, but by love and the blessings that will come from it to not just our families, but to those that may be watching as well.

Personal Reflection Prayer

Lord, I pray that you are my strength in the moments of weakness, for I know that you will still give me what is needed to carry on in the times of struggle. When my family seems to be on unstable grounds, let me be like you and be the solid foundation that is needed. And I will give you the honor and glory. In Jesus' name, Amen.

DAY EIGHTEEN

Don't Quit

Scripture

Galatians 6:9 (NLT) "So let's not get tired of doing what is good. At just the right time we will reap a harvest of blessing if we don't give up."

One of the easiest things to do is quit. It seems to be the fastest way to get rid of headaches, heartaches, frustrations and struggles. Or is it? Think about this: how did you even get here? Not the situation, but the marriage itself. Was it her beauty, was it her affection, was it her love for you, or was it your love for her? I'm guessing it's a combination of them all! Most of all, the love. Now does that Love outweigh whatever it is that you are enduring? Makes you think, right?

Genuine love will have you fighting for dear life for that right one that has come into your life. It reminds you of how you even got there. Now take that and be reminded that God made no mistakes when he joined you two together. So why quit? That's the devil's way out and the way to allow you to miss a major blessing that is surely on the way. So Don't Quit, years from now, you will look back and say remember when, and you will see what you both have come through.

Nothing can separate love that God has put together, it will surely try, but it won't be successful if you remember the original reason: the love that God has for you, your marriage, and your family. Consider it an honor to be tried, for that means God is with you. So, don't quit! God has you covered.

Personal Reflection Prayer

Father, remind me of your purpose that you have for me. You blessed me with this family, and now I pray that you give me the wisdom and guidance now first to seek you and to know that you are in full control. When things are going wrong, bless me with your power to not quit and experience the fullness of the joy of my marriage that you have ordained. In Jesus' name, Amen.

DAY NINETEEN

TEST OF A MAN

Scripture

1 Timothy 6:11 (NLT) "But you, Timothy, are a man of God; so run from all these evil things. Pursue righteousness and a godly life, along with faith, love, perseverance, and gentleness."

You've embarked upon a journey that has had so many twists and turns. Some you expected and some you didn't. Everyone has heard about the drama that comes from the woman's perspective. However, what often gets overlooked is the husband that has gained new children that are not biologically his. These new kids that you now call your own; people often forget that they have fathers. Occasionally, dealing with the children's father comes up. It may be a good experience, but sometimes it's not. The male ego is something that we as men hate to get challenged on. The Test of a Man! The test that comes about your manhood and what you won't be doing to their children. We can prepare for it as men, but are we really prepared for it the way God intended? Let me start by saying that by no means is this an indication of showing cowardness, but a means to stand firm when the devil tries you. As Christians, we are taught to stand boldly on the Word of God whenever we are faced with trials and tribulations, for God will fight our battles. All of this is true and it's a great reference to go by, but we must not also forget the humble but firm approach that is required as well. Pray that God gives you the words as well as the tone when tested. Respect. Pray for it, not only for you to receive, but that you will also recognize that it should be given. When these two roads cross, you can truly see God at work. In almost every battle in the Bible, there was a form of respect from both parties. Until the inevitable occurred. Pray that doesn't have to happen in advance. So when faced with it, God will have already mapped it out for you.

Personal Reflection Prayer

When I am tired, Lord give me strength. When I am weak, make me strong. When I want to give in, help me hold out. Let your power prevail and your love intervene so that I can truly experience the joy you have in store for my family and me. Today and forevermore. In Jesus' name, Amen.

DAY TWENTY

WILL SHE LEAVE ME?

Scripture

Ephesians 5:25 (NLT) "Husbands, love your wives, just as Christ loved the church and gave Himself up for her."

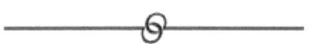

EVERY MAN HAS HAD THIS QUESTION! It's the inevitable question that lingers in our mind when the road gets extremely rocky and you are probably the root cause of it at the time. It's the question that pops up when your past is still lingering in your future and you are fighting hard to fix it. I wish I had a way to truly help stop this question from coming up. I don't have that solution, but I do have a solution. PRAY and WORK. Prayer goes without saying; however, it is the WORK part that I want to help you with. Work will be required to overcome this thought process. It will require work from you to show that your wife also that you are fighting to keep her and keep her happy. Work is not going out and buying things, that's a great gesture, but the Work that we often overlook is our very own actions. What she wants to see is that you are willing to fight for her and with her. She wants to see you standing up for her when the adversaries come. She wants to know that you are on her team.

The Bible says, "He that findeth a wife...Findeth a good thing," and when you find a good thing, sometimes it seems too good to be true - probably prompting the question above. But God basically tells us, you found a good thing and He has blessed it. Now do all that you can to keep her. It's not going to be easy; there will be difficult times that you will have to endure. That is when your real work kicks in. So when this question pops up, it's probably a great indicator that your work may have slipped, and you need to regroup and get back at it. The best way to avoid it: DON'T EVER STOP WORKING! It's an ongoing process from day one. But remember, you are built for it.

Personal Reflection Prayer

Father, you have blessed me with a wife, a good thing that I am pleased to enjoy. Now Lord, equip me with the heart and willingness to want to keep a smile on her face, joy in her heart, and most importantly, praise on her lips. A praise that she gives to you because of your likeness that she sees in me. Bless me to work as the husband and father that you desire me, for my family, as well as myself. In Jesus' name, Amen.

_____
_____
_____
_____
_____
_____
_____
_____
_____
_____
_____
_____
_____
_____
_____
_____

DAY TWENTY-ONE

THE DAYS TO COME

Scripture

Proverbs 27:17 (NLT) "As iron sharpens iron, so a friend sharpens a friend."

As you journey through this relationship/marriage there will be growing pains. A part of me wishes that there was a list of all that we as men will have to endure within a blended family. Since there is not, there is a very favorable direction that you can be pointed in. Walk with God.

There is power in knowing that because you are walking with him, nothing is impossible. Come what may from day to day, God won't lead you wrong. Be slow to speak and quick to listen. We have a listening problem. Let our wives tell us, but if you don't hear anything else, hear what God has to say and what He will have you to do when problems come.

Additionally, you may be blessed enough to where problems are few. Still rejoice because that is God's favor on you. You may be doing everything that God wants you to do within your blended family as a husband and father. Just remember, your blessings could very well be meant to be heard by someone else, even more so another husband or father that needs to hear your success story.

Personal Reflection Prayer

As I travel this journey that you have guided me to, Lord, I pray that you are a lamp unto my feet, a voice in my mind, and a burning in my heart to want to please you and to lead my family to where you like us to go. While I know that trouble will come, remind me that you to have come that I might have life and have it more abundantly. Thank you for what you have done and what you will do in my life as a man, husband, father, and leader. In Jesus' name, Amen.

_____
_____
_____
_____
_____
_____
_____
_____
_____
_____
_____
_____
_____
_____
_____

PART IV

CHILDREN

This section of the devotional will guide you through some of those tough blended family moments when dealing with blending your children.

Our goal is to offer encouragement along with solid Christian-based, real-life application and guidance. Bringing children together can be a daunting task and requires tons of patience, prayer, perseverance and problem-solving. In the beginning, during and continuously pray for your children and with your children. Allow God's love to be the fragrance and spirit within your home.

DAY TWENTY-TWO

WHERE DO I FIT IN?

Scripture

Jeremiah 29:11 (NLT) "For I know the plans I have for you," says the Lord. "They are plans for good and not for disaster, to give you a future and a hope."

Remember when you had to change to a new school or went from elementary, to middle to high school? It was always awkward not knowing what to expect being in a new environment. Will I know where to go? Will I make any new friends? Will I handle the new changes? Will I be able to fit in? If you can remember, it did not happen for the most part overnight. It took some classroom time, hallway time, and time to learn the new teacher and what it all would be like. Question: How did you do? Did you make it? Did you survive? Did you make new friends along with the ones you already had? All of the above questions will come to mind; however, know that it is very similar to a great outcome if you allow it to happen. Maybe it is a new home that you have to live in, maybe it is a new sibling that you now have, and yes even a new bonus parent is now in your life. Make sure you put a positive spin on the questions that you have. Know that you fit in just the same. You are loved more because of the Bonus Parent. (and the extra love that you will receive from all of your new extended family that comes along with them) The environment that you are in, it is still considered a home for you. New siblings will be different (this will take some time) but before you know it, you will have a new person that really has your back. Changes are not always bad; most times changes are for the best. Where do you fit in? Right where you are, nice and snuggled in around a family that loves you more than you know.

Personal Reflection Prayer

God bless me with patience and an open-minded heart. Bless me to see what you are doing and not what I think should be happening. I pray that you guide my heart and thoughts that I can receive the blessings you have for me and my family. Help me to know that you won't lead me wrong. In YOU, I'm am trusting. In Jesus name, Amen.

_____
_____
_____
_____
_____
_____
_____
_____
_____
_____
_____
_____
_____
_____
_____
_____
_____

DAY TWENTY-THREE

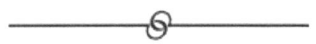

TOGETHER WE MAKE A FAMILY

Scripture

Colossians 2:2 (NLT) "I want them to be encouraged and knit together by strong ties of love. I want them to have complete confidence that they understand God's mysterious plan, which is Christ Himself."

The bringing together of two families requires prayer, dedication and hard work. It may seem that everything is a chaotic mess, and the sense of normalcy is a distant future thought. However, when you stop and focus on what you have around you, you will quickly begin to feel the love of God and love from your family, which will allow everything else to become a blur. The greatest feeling will be knowing and understanding you have all you need when witnessing your family bonding and sticking together. Together following God, your family can do anything. A family that prays together stays together, a family that is together, survives together. Most importantly, together we make a family.

Personal Reflection Prayer

Lord, make us as one family as you desire us to be. When it feels as though we are not on the same page, remind us of your divine guidance of putting us together. Remind us that together we are stronger, together we can overcome anything, and together you will lead us to experience joy, love, peace, and happiness. In Jesus' name, Amen.

_____
_____
_____
_____
_____
_____
_____
_____
_____
_____
_____
_____
_____
_____
_____
_____
_____

DAY TWENTY-FOUR

TRUSTING GOD THROUGH THE PROCESS

Scripture

Matthew 19:26 (NLT) "Jesus looked at them intently and said, 'Humanly speaking, it is impossible. But with God everything is possible.'"

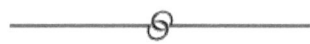

Blending a family is a process and if you are like most of us, it is not easy. This process will require your patience, perseverance, prayers and most of all, the POWER of our almighty God. We must trust God to excel us through the good times, the trying times of joining families. We must trust Him to guide us to properly blend and remain in the midst of our family.

God is the master of our lives and nothing is impossible for Him. When things in our family seem to be out of order, the marriage appears rocky, the kids are unruly and the exes (biological parents) are causing you grief. Remember, nothing is too hard for God. With HIM all things are possible.

Personal Reflection Prayer

For we know through you all things are possible, we pray that your power is felt in our family every day. We pray, Lord, that you be our guide as we build upon the foundation of this union that you have made. When troubles come, guard our hearts and gird our tongues that we can continue to show the love you have given and speak the words of affirmation of the success to come. In Jesus' name, Amen.

_____
_____
_____
_____
_____
_____
_____
_____
_____
_____
_____
_____
_____
_____
_____

DAY TWENTY-FIVE

No Magic Pill

Scripture

Proverbs 18:10 (NLT) "The name of the Lord is a strong fortress; the godly run to him and are safe."

Blending a family and parenting does not come with a rule book and it is definitely a difficult task. As parents, we are tasked with the tiresome job of raising our little ones to grow and become productive citizens of society. When it comes to parenting a blended family, things can be challenging because you are dealing with several different factors. There is no magic pill that will automatically blend your family. The only magic available to you is prayer.

Blending families requires patience, perseverance and prayer. You may become frustrated and tired along the journey of parenting your blended family. Continue to pray and have faith that God will see your family through the difficult times.

Effective Tips To Blend And Parent Your Blended Family

- Stand firmly together and tackle parenting as a unit.

- *You and your spouse should always stand united when it comes to parenting and making decisions.*
- Build a relationship with your children.
- Do not compare siblings
- Host family meetings
  - *Family meetings ensure that everyone receives the same message and allows you to clear up any confusion or misunderstandings immediately.*
  - *Listen and allow everyone to express themselves and be heard.*
- Everyone must abide by the same rules. What is required of one child should be required for them all.
- Clearly define rules and expectations
- Communication is Key
  - *Keep an open line of communication*
  - *Family group chat*
  - *Follow one another on social media platforms (age applicable)*
- Don't be afraid to start over and try again, it will take time to find what works for your family.
- Patience, patience, patience.
  - *Blending your family will require you to practice patience, remain open minded and understanding.*
  - *Integrating families take time to gel.*
- Don't give up

Personal Reflection Prayer

Lord, may all of our efforts to make us become and remain one be successful and pleasing in your site. In Jesus' name, Amen.

DAY TWENTY-SIX

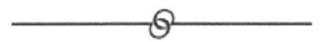

THE TRYING TIMES

Scripture

Colossians 3:14 (NLT) "Above all , clothe yourselves with love, which binds us all together in perfect harmony."

We all know blending anything is not always an easy task. Whether it be food ingredients, drinks, paint or people, it requires a lot of hard work, dedication and patience. When blending families, you will not find an easy button. There is no Ninja, mixer or blender for families, just love, perseverance, and dedication. Blending a family can be taxing, tiring and troublesome. Within blended families, we deal with several external influences that create additional challenges for the household. Some of the trying times we deal with are the ever-changing emotions and attitudes of outside influences that could greatly affect our households. Attempting to bring new people into old places and relationships can cause a great deal of conflict and strife in our households. Sometimes you should remove as many of the outside influences as you possibly can. Your family is a unique blend with a special bond. Work hard during the difficult times to keep the peace within your family. Remember every day is a new day with new grace and new mercy. When things are unbearable or too heavy to carry, hand it over to God and put all your trust in Him to handle it.

When we do not know what to do, He will always have the answer. Let Him take care of it.

Personal Reflection Prayer

Father, the work required of me, helps me do it to the best of my ability. Let your works show forth through my works as I am working to please you and my family. Keep us on one accord that we may feel your presence and that you may be glorified. For through these actions, we know your hand will be busy in our home. In Jesus' name, Amen.

_____
_____
_____
_____
_____
_____
_____
_____
_____
_____
_____
_____
_____
_____
_____

DAY TWENTY-SEVEN

Choosing Sides

Scripture

Exodus 20:12 (NLT) "Honor your father and mother. Then you will live a long, full life in the land the LORD your God is giving you."

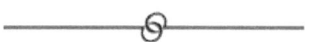

One of the most challenging things to do is to be neutral. Have you tried to keep both of your parents happy, but it gets difficult at times? Even though you have a great time with either parent that you are with, it seems like you get caught in the middle because one parent, or both, might not be okay with the happiness you experience with the other. We get it. This is a hard place to be in. Always remember that this is no reflection of you nor is it your fault. There is comfort in knowing that you don't have to choose a side. Parents can be at odds, but one thing always remains the same; the love that is held for you as their child remains strong. Both parents,-and bonus parents, want to see you happy and do what is best for you. It may not always seem that way; however, it is the truth. One parent may be doing better in life than the other; and remember that it's not your fault for anything that an adult has done. We are taught to honor our mother and our father. God has not put us in a situation to choose by saying that, but in a situation to still enjoy all parents, to include bonus parents. Choosing a side means neglecting one of your parents. Try loving both just the same, try to keep positive attitudes toward both the same.

Personal Reflection Prayer

Lord, I choose you! By choosing you, Lord, I understand that you will give clarity and peace. Keep and place in my heart the desire to continue to love everyone just the same. Help me to know that you haven't taken anything away from me, but you have added to me. Remind me when it gets hard that you said everything works for the good, and I am leaning and trusting you, God, and going to watch it happen. In Jesus' name, Amen.

_____
_____
_____
_____
_____
_____
_____
_____
_____
_____
_____
_____
_____
_____

DAY TWENTY-EIGHT

ALL ABOUT THE KIDS

Scripture

Philippians 2:4 (NLT) "Don't look out only for your own interests, but take an interest in others, too."

When you blend an abundance of things you are no longer able to see individual characteristics, a blended family is no different. It is imperative to ensure that there is union throughout the family, and everyone has a role and a VOICE. Blending families, personalities, baby mamas, baby daddies, ex-wives, and ex- husbands is no easy task; you will simply need plenty of prayer, patience and occasionally spirits to get you through some days. That may be the Holy Spirit or liquid spirits!

Most importantly, remember this is the life YOU chose and although you may be happy, you must work even harder to ensure the happiness of your children. They did not choose your new spouse. If children had a choice, they would choose for their biological parents to be together. As an adult, remember although you are aware of all the negative things that may rub you the wrong way about your ex, your child/children only know them as the person they love and cherish, which is mom or dad to them. Ask yourself can you mask your negative feelings for the wellbeing of your child/children?

I pray that your answer is yes. If not, you have some work to do. Start with prayer and self-reflection. Once you work on self, you can move to the other parties within the family. Growth comes from within.

Personal Reflection Prayer

Help me accept change, Lord, help me lead by your thoughts and not thoughts of my own. Help me to remove myself to be effective in understanding my family members. Happiness is my heart's desire, and with your guidance I know that I can fully achieve it. Bless me to accept the new and the changes that are being made in my life. In Jesus' name, Amen.

_____
_____
_____
_____
_____
_____
_____
_____
_____
_____
_____
_____
_____
_____
_____
_____
_____

PART V

WE ARE ONE

This section of the devotional is dedicated to the entire family. Once you all have joined together in holy matrimony, it is time to work on gelling and blending your family. Prayerfully you have been working on blending your family prior to the marriage. When you are dating one another it is imperative that you date the children as well. Remember there is no magic pill that will automatically blend your family because you have said "I Do". It will take time and a lot of work for the families to come together. Remain intentional in your communication, and intentional in your love for one another. Focus on your family, write your own blended family story and do not allow society or outsiders to define your family.

DAY TWENTY-NINE

MATCHING HEARTS

Scripture

Matthew 6:21 (NLT) "Wherever your treasure is, there the desires of your heart will also be."

One important factor is that what is in your heart about your spouse speaks volumes. The way your heart feels is the driving force behind a lot of things that you do for one another. When you have two hearts joined together, determined to accomplish the same thing, that is an unstoppable combination.

Matching hearts are considered to be two like-minded, loving, caring, and determined couples that have made up minds that nothing shall separate them. Who know that what God has joined together nothing can put asunder.

Ensure that your hearts match first and foremost. Once this goal is accomplished, it doesn't matter what may come your way, together you can overcome and achieve anything. Matching hearts that are following God surely can't fail. Where is your treasure after God? If your spouse is your first response, then the desire to make sure they are happy is probably already there. If not, then think about prioritizing and putting them right after God. See what new joys and level of happiness that you can enjoy.

Personal Reflection Prayer

Lord mend our hearts as one as Husband and Wife and as a family. Through the love in our hearts, help us pour out into each other the love and compassion that you continuously show us. Your love grants peace, power, and the willingness to forgive, and we pray that you allow those same traits to be shown and acted out through us towards one another. In Jesus' name, Amen.

_____
_____
_____
_____
_____
_____
_____
_____
_____
_____
_____
_____
_____
_____
_____
_____

DAY THIRTY

Blended And Loving It

Scripture

Romans 8:28 (NLT) "And we know that God causes everything to work together for the good of those who love God and are called according to His purpose for them."

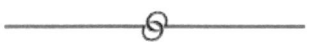

Blending a family is not an easy task. It's not something that you can walk into and take lightly. There are so many contributing factors from within and outside your home that you must contend with to make it truly work. One thing that can be learned is that you must have patience. Know that God didn't put you in the situation for nothing; there is a reason your hearts found each other - so that they can work together for His purpose. For example, when you are baking a cake, if you attempted to eat each ingredient individually, you would probably not like the taste of some ingredients very well. However, when the time is taken and each different ingredient is mixed together, you start to get a sneak peek of what is to come. The smell of the mixture starts to catch your nose, and even the taste of the mixture has changed to something that makes you want to lick the bowl. Finally, the result of a great tasting cake is what you get after putting in the work to blend it all. Same thing applies to a blended family. Some ingredients if dealt with alone might not be all that good; however, when you take that ingredient and mix it with other ingredients, what you will end up getting is something that will come together beautifully. May not have tasted great getting there, may even had to put in a little more elbow grease to get some of the lumps out. But once put through the fire and functioning as one, what you get is a perfect blend. Or better yet, you will find yourself... "Blended and Loving It!" Set your family goals and write your own blended family story.

Personal Reflection Prayer

As we look forward to the next days and years to come, Lord, please be our guide and let your love and grace be felt as we move to build upon what you have designed. Blend us as one, that we can combat anything that the enemy may try to do. We thank you for all that you have done and what you are going to do. In Jesus' name, Amen.

_____
_____
_____
_____
_____
_____
_____
_____
_____
_____
_____
_____
_____
_____
_____
_____
_____
_____
_____
_____

About the Authors

"What God has joined together let no man put asunder!" This has been the marital phrase to live by. However, what happens when what God is joining together consists of more than two ingredients? Well, you get us!! Years ago, God merged two families together and created His greatest Blend ever. He and his two, met Her and her two, and became One in Holy Matrimony. Through the love and care for one another, Ours was added to the mix. Although we are not biologically connected, everyone became OURS! We are a family that you will never see division or different treatment in our home. Although we are not the traditional family, we are one family. We are all a part of the body of Christ, we are all Christians and one body. We operate under this format and most importantly keep God first and foremost in all that we do. When you blend something together you are unable to see separation. That is our mentality with our family. We are blended and joined together with LOVE, or as we like to call it, "Blended and Loving It"!

Dr. & Mrs. Wright

Dr. Slavoski L. Wright Sr. Bio

Slavoski Wright is a lifelong resident of Texas. By the guidance and calling of God some nineteen years ago, he began preaching the gospel. Slavoski strengthened his foundation by gaining a bachelor's and master's degree in Christian Ministry from Wayland Baptist University. He also holds a Doctoral degree in Divinity from North Central Theological Seminary.

Through the grooming and preparation of his grandfather, he was able to become the gospel minister that he is today. God has seen fit that he would serve Him by leading His people in the capacity over the course of time as an Associate Pastor, Youth Pastor and Assistant Pastor in local churches.

Slavoski loves to help equip people to have a better walk with Christ and strengthen families, especially blended families. Additionally, Slavoski gives a living example through his own blessing of a family with his, as he calls her, missing rib (Umeka) and six wonderful children. Kori, Slavoski II, Hannah, Braylon, Ryan and Dixon. Slavoski is also a member of Alpha Phi Alpha Fraternity, Inc. where he serves as a Chaplain.

Umeka D. Wright Bio

Umeka Wright, MA, is an author, blogger, wife, and mom. Between her and her husband Rev. Slavoski L. Wright Sr., they parent six children - two college-aged children, two high schoolers, one middle schooler, and a toddler. Professionally, Umeka is a school counselor specializing in adolescent and teen substance abuse prevention and interventions.

As an outlet to share her grows and glows of blending two very different families, in 2012, Umeka began the blog Blended & Loving it. Focused on bringing unity, Blended & Loving It is an online community for all mothers, bonus moms, stepmoms, bio moms, and soon to be stepmoms to collaborate, motivate, educate, and encourage one another. Her direct experience brings about the substance you can rely on to aid in the heartaches, headaches, and rewarding times of your family becoming one.

Connect with Umeka by visiting her blog, Blended And Loving It www.blendedandlovingit.com

www.ingramcontent.com/pod-product-compliance
Lightning Source LLC
Chambersburg PA
CBHW021914180426
43198CB00035B/562